CAN YOU DO WHAT
BEARDED DRAGONS
DO?

written by Stevie Buzbee

illustrated by Jonathan Antonio

**To all the dragons
who have touched my life.**

This dragon's name is Smaug.
She loves to wave hello!

Can you wave hello to Smaug?

Bearded Dragons can be a lot of different colors. They can be yellow, brown, white, red, and even orange! Stubby is more of a yellow color, and Balerion is more orange.

Can you point to your favorite color in this room?

Just like us, Bearded Dragons grow very fast when they're young. Look how big Blackbeard got in only one year! He is 1.5 feet long now.

Can you show how big that is?

This is Stubby. She likes reading about things other dragons do.

Can you read this sentence with Stubby? "The small brown dragon reads stories about her friends."

8

Dragons love trying different foods. They love meats, sweets, and a lot of other treats!

What new foods do you want to try?

This is Blackbeard's mad face. When he's angry, his beard turns dark black, which is where he got his name!

Can you show Blackbeard your best mad face?

Even dragons need baths sometimes.

What is your favorite thing about bath time?

Dragons enjoy playing in the sand.
Sometimes they even bury themselves in it!

What is your favorite thing to do?

One day a feather fell from the sky and it scared poor Blackbeard! When dragons are scared, they either run and hide, or puff up big with their mouth open! Blackbeard is trying his best to stay brave.

Can you show Blackbeard your brave face to give him courage?

Dragons can fall asleep in some pretty unusual places—tucked under a blanket, snuggling with a buddy, or even upside down!

Can you pretend to be asleep like a dragon?

20

Everyone feels sad sometimes, even dragons. They feel better when they're with their friends and family! Blackbeard and Puff always comfort each other.

Who do you talk to when you feel sad?

Dragons have best friends too! Smaug
and Billy Bird love to share salads.

What do you and your best friend
like to do together?

Dragons love sports too!

Can you pretend to swing a bat like Puff?

Dragons love the holidays! They love getting spooky for Halloween, and also jolly with the Christmas spirit!

What do you like most about celebrating holidays?

It's time for the dragons to go now.
Goodbye until next time!

Can you wave goodbye to Smaug?

About the Author

Stevie Buzbee is a writer and animal enthusiast based in Pasadena, California. She shares her life with a loving husband, crotchety bird, and a few sweet bearded dragons. She enjoys beach life, mountain time, lounging with friends, and most of all, being lazy. Her writing is derived from real life experiences...and a little imagination.

About the Illustrator

Jonathan Antonio is a Filipino Graphic Artist. He is a family man with two lovely daughters. He also shares his home with his beloved dogs and adorable hamsters. He enjoys making people laugh, bodybuilding, music and singing. He uses a "pen and pencil" tablet to bring his illustrations to life. Currently, he works as a freelance artist and Professional Editorial Cartoonist in the Philippines.

CPSIA information can be obtained
at www.ICGtesting.com
Printed in the USA
BVHW052202200720
584027BV00001BA/1